*A dedication to my ex-wife
For giving birth to my new life.*

Les,
You are a real one!!
Thank you for the support.
I hope these black pages bring light to your life.

—Tai

# (HER)

by tonii

**NOW**LEDGE
PUBLISHING

*(HER)* Copyright © 2019 by tonii

All rights reserved. No part of this book may be reproduced in any form or by any electronic or mechanical means, including information storage and retrieval systems, without permission in writing from the author or publisher, except for the use of brief quotations in a book review.

Nowledge Publishing
New York, NY

www.toniiinc.com

Illustration and cover design by tonii

**ISBN: 978-10928435-1-5**

Birth (1-25)

Adolescence (27-57)

Growth (59-97)

Death (99-163)

Revelation (165-205)

Resurrection (207-251)

Anew (253-277)

Redefine (279-297)

...

*Poem Titles (299-313)*

*Read carefully
Let each poem absorb in
So you can
Understand* Her.

Birth

I loved Her
No, I love Her.

Sincerly,
I, *Her lover*

I am not a human
I am Her man
Her, being a woman
I am foreign
In this land of men
An alien
From a distant planet
Dispatched to be Her man
Among humans.

Just from a look
I want to read your book

The melaninated cover cements
My desire to explore its contents

The simplicity of its design went
Unnoticed, but I realized the intent

I follow the title and your name
Along the spine
I flip it over to observe it's behind

I notice the details
In the placement of the title
I realize the sanctity of this manuscript

It is your bible

The complexity within its pages
Is contrasted by the external simplicity
That Leaves no traces

It smiles at me
As its pearly white letters glow
I now want to open it and let it show

Everything that I can discover
Just know:

You had me hooked
From the cover

Of your book.

Life is green
A voyage along an internal stream

A path that bleeds
If purpose is not received

Pink pastures constrict
And flushes out all of it.

A dot is where I began
And a dot is where I will end
A dot into lines
And lines give life to shape
As they bend.

Embodies rage, land, water
And life in Her girth
In the span of Her arms
She consumes the dead
To make way for birth.

You're beautiful
God dipped his paint brush
Into the hue of the sky at Dawn
Then masterfully painted
Your complexion
Onto your bones
You're beautiful.

Blue collapse
Creates a white line

That lives until
It reaches the Shoreline

Dividing the hues
Of multiple blues

The peace I feel
From my views

Staring out into the abyss,
The sea

I am greeted by Her
As she waves at me.

Rising above a line of separation
After living my life in the night
It seems I have obtained my imagination
As my heart awakens from your light

I want nothing else in this life
But to wake and find you near
I know that all days are not always bright
But with you I do not fear

You are the sign that I am alive
You radiate life within my inner parts
I have lived unsatisfied and deprived
As I walked within my days of dark

A new day presents a new way
For you to show me your all
And today is our day
So no longer shall we stall

I ask that you rise and never set on me
Trap me with you on the horizon
Just be next to me and step with me
Always give me your morning glow to rise in

Bright you are and will remain
Faithful will be our bond
The sun and you are one and the same
My day begins with you, my Dawn.

Looking you in your hazel eyes
I see my reflection
Your carmel skin glistens
Wrapped in my arms
You are protected.

It's the look
In your eyes
When you're
Passing by
Your lips
Say, "hi"
It gets
Me high

It's the scent
Of your fumes
Your smile
It blooms
And fills
The room
I'm into You

My friend and Lady
Here it goes again
Let's be lovers
More than friends
Last forever
Never end
Combined together
By the hands

Picture this
It's you
And me
Making our way
Into ecstasy
My dream
Is you being
Eternally
With me.

I can't wait until we are
Face to face
Eyes into eyes
Lips to ears
As ears hear voice
Hands reaching for hands
Thoughts rushing in minds
Smiles showing signs
As time recedes from existence

Attraction igniting flames
Hearts beating simultaneously
As conversations lead to laughter
History
Intellect
Memories
Past
And present

Contact first from eyes
Then hands
Then bodies
With hugs
Fulfilling all of our expectations
Ending our anxiety
Being able to now use all of my senses

Smell your perfume
Applied right after your shower
Hear your voice
That was trapped in my cellular speaker
See the face
That remained still in the photos you sent
Touch the hands
That typed in all of our conversation
And then taste
Every flavor your body leaks
I will let my imagination continue to speak
Until the day we actually meet.

# Adolescence

When I fly to you
You fly from me
We fly between
The branches life leaves

And when I leave
Who would believe
We would long for our next flight
Far more than can be conceived

When you fly to me
I fly from you
The distance causes
Everything to feel anew

And when you leave
I feel deceived
For I wanted
It to last for eternity

When I fly from you
And you fly from me
We fly towards the sun
As it is setting and rising

But when I fly to you
And you fly to me
Our flight will no longer be in the skies
Because we will fly inside of each other
Like butterflies.

I met Her at a cafe
Between red and blue

The streets were all black
Freshly paved and new

I entered into the door
Which read "yellow cafe"

It was three squares away
From where she stayed

I saw Her there
Sitting solemnly at a table square

She stared out of the window
As I appeared

Looking up at me
She begins to smile

Wearing Mondrian
I love Her style.

I wake up everyday at 3 am sharply
With you on my mind
You ask me how I slept
I respond, "Hardly"
Partly, because of the impression
You made in me
Continued to push its way
Into my flesh
After we left
That rooftop
...
I can't stop
Thinking of you
Your smile
Your eyes
Your natural hair
I'm still up there
While you are now in here
And what began that night
Has not stopped
It continues everyday
Again and again
Sharply,
At 3 am.

Your lips press against mine
And the red tinted cover
Transfers onto me
As my lips now wear your color.

Her true self is buffering
Download will begin shortly
Control-alt-delete
...
I always restart
Before the download completes.

When I look into your eyes
I get high

I lay down on the moon
Watching the clouds passing by

From hours until days
Then days turn into nights

You don't escape my mind
No matter how hard you try

I inhale you

Then exhale too

You fill up my lungs
I feel something is going on

I keep giggling
Trembling
Smiling
Then, crying

My emotions are steering me wrong
I'm going up.

She's divine
Her movements seem to halt time
That time that intertwines
Reality with dreams
Dreams wait for me to approach
Like mines
To then explode
Into my heart's design
To capture my mind
She's fine
As a bottle of the finest italian wine
As she shines
Like silver chains
Dangling outside in a sunny rain
Causing a sudden change
Igniting my burning flame
Ridding me of my burden pains
Her skin glistens
Like a waxed surface
And nourishes
The hunger of my sights
She dims my global light
Then enlightens me
To Her exquisite impression
The confession of my lust
Crusted over my heart
Paralyzes my body parts
Beautiful she is
While she passes like the wind
And like the wind
She comes and goes
So I know
I shall see Her again.

Although we are miles apart
Our hearts live on the horizon

Into the sky we fly to meet
At the first appearance of the sunshine's peek

It's in your smile and in your eyes
That I have found a place to dwell

But in the same manner that you rise
You now disappear from me as well.

The way I call you all the time
Is like a fish on your line
Reel me in
Pull me in
Then
...
Take me out of the ocean.

You're beautiful
From the moment you rise
Until the moment you set
Under covers and sheets
You radiate in my life
You're beautiful

Missing you
Right now
Wishing you
Were here
Remembering when
You were
Being impatient
Until the next time
Wanting you
More than ever
Reminiscing
On how you felt
Seeing you
With my eyes closed
Needing you
Right now.

When it's cold outside
I can be your heat.

Winter
Snow
Spring
Returns
Summer
Burns
Fall
In love
With me.

From your beach
I take some sand

I place it in
A jar and then

Whenever I want
To relive again

The moments we shared
The places we've been

I pour your sand
In my hand

And then
I'm there with you again.

My sea is within your ocean
Your river flows into my lake
My puddle is consumed by your pond
Your marsh is within my swamp
My rain falls into your gulf
Your snow melts inside of my pool
My spring leads into your canal
Your stream runs off of my waterfall.

When I was in Her
She was on me
I was writer
She was loose leaf
I was on Her
She breathed deeply
I was fire
She was cool breeze
I was with Her
She was with me
I was tired
She rest assured me
I held tighter
She gripped me tightly
I was sailor
She was blue sea
I went deeper
She received gladly
When I was in Her
She was all things
I was all Her
And she was all me.

Growth

You love me
You hate me
You want me
You don't
You heal me
You break me
You will promise
You won't.

I met Her in the winter
In Her eyes was the summer
When she smiled it was Fall
Because she made me fall under

Her kiss was the Spring
I was sprung yearlong
When she was in pain, it was rain
Hurricane, winds strong

When I leave Her, leaves changed
When she goes, white snow
Her wind is wild, never tamed
Her grass always grows

Clear skies when she's happy
Thunderstorms when she's not
Full moon when she's napping
Rainbow when Her rain stops

Her weather is ever changing
However Her nature calls
Whether she is sunny or rainy
I will love Her through it all.

She hates me
Argues and debates me
Aches me
Forsakes me
Mends me
Breaks me
Remakes me
Takes me
Creates me
Then I hate Her.

That smile
Those lips
That a**
Those eyes
That laugh
Those feet
That p*ssy
Those kisses
That body
Those memories
That look
Those f*cks
That love
Those days
That feeling
With Her.

Against the odds that faced us
We believed in something few speak of
Knowing that judgement
Could come on a daily basis
We had the audacity to love

From the start
We knew this would be different
We knew the stakes at hand
While the world around
Would not accept our love
We still stood hand in hand

As time went by and together we grew
Weeds were in between our branches
The more we wanted happiness
Selfishness infested our circumstances

We soaked ourselves in weedicide
Hoping that it would remedy
Contemplated homicide and suicide
From the depth of our audacity

We shed some problems
Some were new
While others were relentless
Regrets were brewing, failure approaching
Testing whether ours love's authentic

Together we started
And together we went
Through weather
Regardless of the world's 2 cents

We had the audacity
To believe in the unconventional
That true love should be us together
Being pure and more than sensual

Fertilized by truth
We grew together in the physical
Metaphysical, mental, intellectual
Biological and the spiritual

This relationship has permanence
That can't be comprehended in the visual
Our hearts were invested as capital
To fund a unity that guarantees residuals

We are no longer individuals
We have intertwined in our existence
We knew exactly what we wanted
And in each other is where it existed

From our first hug and our very first kiss
I knew we were meant to be because
We shared in a joint audacity
This great audacity

To love.

You are beautiful
Like a flower, you bloom in our bedroom
Your pedals falling onto the floor
Now bare
You are beautiful.

1, 2, 3
Her, me, and she
We three
L, O, V, E.

Look into me
And see inside of you

Your exterior
Is my interior
My red within your blue

Speak into my ear
And listen for the echoes
In your heart beat

Your thoughts are my reality
Time folds on itself
We are entangled so deep

I can't escape

Who I am

Vanishes without a trace.

I gave them
The other half of me
It really wasn't bad, you see
Because for my half
They both gave me a half
So I now have a whole
Plus the half of me.

When I'm not in front of you
I'm working for you
When I'm not talking with you
I'm talking about you
When I'm not around you
I'm hoping to be
But actually
I am there
Because I gave you a part of me

When I am not showing my love to you
I'm thinking of how to
When I'm not teaching you
I'm learning from you
When I'm not laughing with you
Thoughts of you make me laugh at you

I live in this world
My world is you
You are my reasons
And this poem is for you two.

I am them
They are me
She is Her
Her is she
I and she are Her
Her and I are she
Her and she is I
She and Her are me

I am them
They are me
Her, she, and I are we
We are me, Her, and she
We are Her
We are she

We are one
But we are three.

Simultaneously
In unison we
Produce harmony
As we arrive concurrently
When you cum with me.

Window pain
Glass stained blue
Drained my blood
Tears flood because of you

Reflecting the sky
Forecast is clear
The ocean's current
Determines when we are near

Remorse is my complexion
Grief in my melanin
Sorrowfully melancholy
Depression in my skeleton

Sapphire's hue
Cobalt state of being
Persistent despondency
I am indigo from you leaving.

I can't keep my hands off of you
It's a magnetic attraction that pulls me to
Your skin is conductive
My energy accrued

I can't keep my eyes off of you too
Your image is burned in my retina's view
You have permanence in my optics
A visual glue

I can't keep my lips off of you
I continuously kiss your light, melaninated hue
Naturally our lips meet like the clouds kiss blue

I can't keep my mind off of you
My thoughts are reruns of what I would do
If you were here with me
And I was there with you

I can't keep me off of you
It's a continuous war trying to separate us two
It's like, we are branded by each other
Being each other's tattoos

Even though it seems we may be taboo
I can't seem to keep my life away from you
...
And honestly,
I don't want to.

Cutting through the sea
You are able to remain stable
As waves are created on both sides of my heart
Circumstances hitches behind your path
But I extend them outwardly
They Dissipate
Away from you
And away from me

My sea was calm and undisturbed
Until you came across me
It is now restless
I guess this is
How it is intended to behave
When you are salvation for someone
Who needs to be saved

Or a means of transportation
For someone trying to reach their destination

Although forces have attempted
Their destruction on your boat
I have assisted in keeping your vessel afloat

I am a vital component to your life's design
That gives you the ability to go far
Above my sea you are
Seen for your beauty and your feats
But I have prevented you from sinking
In life's deep
As I have existed beneath.

The eyes have never lied
And the heart is never satisfied

...

Until I met you.

I stare into your eyes
As you stare back into mine
And time elapses
Just like waves collapsing
On the Atlantic shore
Our love is lead by the Titantic's ore
Taking our heart on an romantic tour
As the music rains in a frantic pour
Across our vast land
And my hand
Gently runs across your skin
Then my lips softly disperses onto you
As the gentle sound of my voice
Moves through you
And you move your head
Slightly to the left
And my lips kiss your neck
And your eyes are kept Closed
...
(Deeply inhale and exhale)
...
Who knows where this mood is going to take us
And who knows what kind of things
We are going to make
But, I'm hoping that it is love
I'm hoping that this is love
Because I will treat you like Queen Nefertiti
Reading your body
Seeing that your body needs me
To take hold of and fold
My arms around and control
And abound in your life
Be around when things are not right
Be the bright sun for your daylight

And the moon's glow
Through your gloomy nights
My delight is upon the honey
That rest on your lips
The sweetness of your kiss touches my tongue
And the bliss numbs my movement
Creating a soothing sense of comfort
And my thoughts wonder
Wondering how it would be
If I was under you
Or you were under me
Or little things like
If I was that drop of water
Dripping down your chest
From the melted piece of ice
In the heat of the summer
I wonder or dream of
Being a drop of your lipgloss
As you apply me on your lips
Then, evenly spread me across
Or if I was something that you lost
In your back pocket
...
I wish I was your shower faucet
As my love showers over your bareness
Giving awareness to your natural image
I would want for my name
To come from your mouth like the sentence
"I love you"
Or just being the instance in time
When time is not a worry
Or being treasure that you bury
In your fleshly soil
Or being like a python
Constrict and coil around your entire body

Or being the oil that runs
The engine in your autobody
I'm thinking probably this is love
Others say it's an infatuation
The lust for you burns inside of me
Even in our conversation
The complications you are causing within me
Is sort of bitter but still sweetly experienced
We're friends but I want intimate
I want to walk with you on a infinite journey
Sleep in the same bed at night
And rise together early in the morning
I need you, I'm addicted
I want to preserve you, like hot tea
And just sip it
Yes, I want to sip you
Please listen
I submerge in a tub filled to the rim
With pictures of you
And on each picture
I wrote the words "I love you"
I bath with them
Because you are what makes me clean
Truthfully, you are my entirety
You are my omni
You are the reason for my existence
So as I watched you walk down that isle
The ring, your vows, and your beautiful smile
Your dress and that kiss
Confirmed my decision the best
The homicide committed
From his lips receiving my kiss
Sends me to my eternal form
...
As the razor slides across my wrist.

Death

The spectrum of my gradient
Goes from light to the dark
Within, I'm night
But outwardly radiant
Deep in my emotions swimming with sharks

I've chosen my hue
In the same manner that I selected you
Happiness gradually descends to pain
And my blues went from being light
To deeper blue
While my forecast is eternal rain

White
Light gray
Gray
Dark gray
Black
I have been them all
Life was once bright
But now it is something it lacks
...
As all light in my life dissolves.

The sun rose over the horizon
Then suddenly set in the east
Day never became day
And my night never ceased.

Where is the sun?
It is Dawn
I looked forward to its shine
But there is none
It is gone
It has vanished
It disappeared
No day
No night
No time
Just here.

I want you to touch me
The way you once touched me
Upon a time

When you let your finger tips
Glide over my abdomen
And along my spine

Our skin melted from our body heat
Like chocolate
As your skin pressed up
Against mine

We touched each other
Once upon a time

I want you to kiss me
The way your lips once kissed me
Upon a time

When you kissed my lips
My neck, chest, abdomen
And my shaft
All in a straight line

Your lips were soft and plump
As you applied gloss
And a lipstick the color
Of red wine

We kissed each other
Once upon a time

I want you to hold me
The way your arms once held me
Upon a time

Like on those cold nights
Under the moonlight
How your body wrapped around me
Like wild vines

Your hands would hold me tightly
When I was on your insides
As your heart rate increased
And the pleasure climbed

We held each other
Once upon a time

I want you to be to me
What you were once to me
Upon a time

Making me laugh
And bringing me joy
My life was at its prime

Your mind stimulated my thoughts
Your eyes were my muse
And your smile was my sunshine

You were everything to me
And my life was complete
At least
Once
Upon a time.

My life was full of empty bottles
As I choked on the pain
That you fed me constantly
Too much to swallow
No way to breathe
I wish I had something to wash this down
But you also drank the life out of me.

Her intention was not to begin bartending
But she sat down
On both ends of the bar counter
And began spending
Her time
Her soul
Her life
She paid the price for those martinis
As the glass continually sunk to half empty
But half full is what she kept seeing
Looking up
Head back constantly
Because that's the only way to find a remedy
Or make the contents of the bottles
Transfer life from being a complex reality
Into lucid dreams
Moments seemed
To bleed into weeks and internally
Weeks bled into months of the same things
Vodka met Gin
Gin met Rum
No drop of them left behind
Until the bottle is done
Until the battle is won
Until the pain is numb
Or until the trigger is pulled on
Leaving a familiar limpness
And red contents gone
An empty ~~bottle~~ body
Lay next to a gun.

I live in Her
She died in me
As I leave
She is empty.

I only have half of me
I gave the other half to she.

The burning flame
Consumes our love
Disintegrating
What it once was
The ashes then added
To an urn labeled
"My first loves."

Standing within the fire
My feet are scorched
At every flicker of these flames

As the raging hues of red, orange, and yellow
Consume my vision
I have discovered this rage
Within the perimeter of my own flesh

I've found the gates of perdition
And I have entered into the province of Lucifer

I have been conceived by wickedness
And shaped by the palms of wretchedness

I've left the heavens to now wallow in hell

It's impurity feeds me
Like the breast of a diseased mother

As I am comforted by the arms
Of a decrepit soul
I dissolve in my despondency

And any sanctity that I may have retained
Since the fall
Has now evaporated into nothingness

I am evil.

I hate that I loved you
I love that I hate you
A perspective
I can't ignore

I despise that I adored you
I adore that I despise you
It helps me
Not think of you
Anymore.

It was beauty
When I met Her
(Augmented)

I wore Her
To look better
(Complemented)

Solid gold?
Felt real
(Authentic)

Fit perfect
Around my neck
She glistened

Pressure started
Revealing everything
Hidden

She was yellow
But on the inside
Argentic

Then, turmoil, chaos
Rain and storms came
(Hectic)

I took Her off of my neck
It was green
(Synthetic).

You could have never told me
She wasn't meant for me
Until she said it.

I looked into the mirror
And no one was there

Not your face
Not your eyes
Not your hair

I walked a little closer
Still no one appeared

Only emptiness
Loneliness
Pain and fear

The mirror that once had a beautiful reflection
Full of my happiness
My joy
My cheer

Is now bare
Because my reflection
Was a woman
I loved
That disappeared.

What use is a mirror that provides no reflection
But only to break it
And use its pieces for dissection
My wrist can use an incision
My heart has been neglected
So I can use one of these shards to eject it
Take it out of my chest
In the same manner she departed out of my life
This mirror seems to be useful
In dealing with my strife
My adam's apple
Is a great location for
Cutting across
...
My voice is lost
As my body paints the kitchen floor
Red.

Speak no evil
Hear no evil
See no evil
Because
Together
We are evil.

There is a right and a wrong way
To do wrong

There is a right and a wrong way
To do right

There is a right and wrong way to live

There is no right or wrong way for Her to die.

She took my drink
I was still quinched
She took my money
Down to my last cent
She took my calm
Made me feel tense
She took my mass
I remained dense
She tried to invade
I put up my defense
She took my love
Only in the past tense
She huffed and puffed
I was made of cement
She took me with Her
With malicious intent
She dissemble my life
I had to reinvent
She took my choices
I was forced to consent
Then she took my children
And finally
...
She made a dent.

Darkened within
This hostile environment
Screaming and yelling
In all conversations
Suicide in discussions
Within the place that I reside in
Arguing and cursing
As my children's views
Are sculpted within their eyelids
Full bottles acquired by debits
Contents deposited
Vanished into Her body
Evanescence of liquid pain
The degradation
And separation of a coalescence
My family stained
By red wine
Traveling down the esophagus
Intoxicated by design
To create an individual
Who is disinclined to change
But blame is distributed outwardly
While life is lived haphazardly
I am accused of reacting cowardly
Towards absurdities that occurs
But before I lose my sanity
Or the control of my destiny
I utilize my ability
To let go of Her.

Have you ever?
Looked at the love of your life
Lie limp and unresponsive
When you call Her name
No response returns
Not because she is sleep
Nor because she did not hear you
But because the goose was grey
And the rock was named Sir
And she had a friend named Gin
And now all of them
Have robbed Her of Her consciousness

Have you ever?
Watched someone's life decompose
Like a roadkill carcass on your bedroom floor
Empty of everything you loved about your life
Your happiness
Your experiences
Your smiles and laughter
And you are forced to watch it
Lay empty
Like the bottle laying beside Her

Both lying on a cold tiled floor
While your heart palpitates
At rates faster than it has ever done before
Your mind racing at a sprinter's pace
As you chase reasons
And your attention is coming and leaving
As you look over your shoulder
And see your daughter's face
Looking at Her mother
Through the crack of the door

Have you ever?
Witnessed self inflicted pain
Or had your eyes stained with the images
Of blood leaking out of the body
You once kissed
You once made love with
And no matter how much you squeeze
The liquid keeps running out of Her wrist
No one knows the trouble I feel
Unless you have had the most unluckiest fate
To experience this


Have you ever?
Wanted someone to live
Way more than they would like to
And the more you do
The more you change
The conclusions seems the same:
The blame always falls on you


Have you ever?
Faced a reality
Where you had to make a decision
That would cause the pain of a large incision
Within the chest of your children's body
But you knew that it is better
Than your children eventually finding
Their mother's body
Lying on your bedroom floor
Embodying the change
To their childhood stories
Never being happily ever after any more
Like all of the stories you've read to them before

Have you ever?
Had to endure such
A self inflicted unnatural disaster
Ending with internal bleeding and life receding
And no one believing
That this could have ever happened

Have you ever?
Left because it was the only option
That left you not incarcerated
Her not incapacitated
And your children not deteriorated
But your home would be incinerated
And the more time you spend contemplating
The more she keeps intoxicating
So you turn to your poetry
And write how you feel
Being the only thing availble to deal
With life this real

Have you ever?

...

Because I have.

She was so pretty
She raped my life
Her smile radiated over me
Burnt me twice
Her touch was like molten lava
That scorched my soul
She invaded my world
And took control
It was something I said
I would always avoid
To give so much of myself
To then end
Destroyed.

F*ck Her,

Sincerly,
Her F*cker.

You were perfect

...

At doing exactly what it took
To make me want to leave
And not give a f*ck.

Shackles clamped around my mind
Darkness surrounds as I try to find
Vision inside of this chamber of mine
But what I have found is
I'm surrounded by defeat
Being whipped by deceit
Bars enclose this self-disposed,
Guilty clothed soul
Being a product of the decisions
That I have chosen
These chains hang and clang
At my every attempt of escape
Down here, I have been beaten
Interrogated
And raped
I no longer dream of my life's great victories
I now long for death
Longing to rest peacefully
Somewhere in history
But I also long for light
Despite all of the other amenities life grants
Light seems to be one of my greatest priorities
And being given the chance
To receive just a glimpse of where I am
Can begin my navigation
And development of a plan
Light provides a resource that creates vision
But darkness covers me and I lack ambition
I have been self-captured, self-inflicted
Self-defined, self-descriptive
Self-imprisoned, self-envisioned
Selfishly enslaved because fear has risen
Given a place to reside
Inside of this dungeon of mind.

I want to whisper all the things
That are within my core
To make sure that I'm empty before
I find out what my life is for
Sure, I love you
But there's more beyond this
Cliché ritual or habitual statement
In fact, I adore you
Metaphorically, you are the sand on my shores
And my waves beat upon you
Like the constant rhythm in my veins
Moving my adoration from my muscular
To my mental and mental to spiritual
My thoughts sail on memories
Like the pilgrims navigation
Across the seven seas
And even heaven sees
The constancy of my heart's concentration
You're consecrated
Set apart
Elevated
Everyone else is lessened

You were my queen
Others were peasants
You were a blessing to me
Divinely created
With all of my bare necessities
You were the perfect meal for me
With a balanced recipe
Successfully I have seen miracles
Just having you to share
My marital experience with
Was like the lips of a god upon my life
Giving me a breathgiving kiss
And this is not all
There are infinite pages to this list
Just take for instance
Your smile
Like a parent to a child
I tried to nurture it
I tried to groom your lips just for this
With the influence of each and every kiss

...

But it wasn't enough
And all of this
I will truly miss.

How could I ever pick up
The million broken pieces
From my shattered heart?

You ask me to use glue
To mend the fragments together
After you have spread them apart

Even if I was capable
Or equipped to mend all of it
I would never be the same

I would still have a million different
Weaknesses and reasons
To remember the pain

I am damaged
And can't manage to find
A solution for this

I've concluded
It would be an illusion to think
That I could ever forgive and forget

It would take a million years
And a million tears
From your life and your eyes

But you don't have enough time
To do neither with me
So goodbye.

I apologize
That I couldn't disguise lies
And always strived to give you
The truth untied
And tried my best
To keep your dreams alive

Please pardon me
For my courtesy
Of placing your needs
Above what I needed
As I pleaded
While your greediness
Exceeded
Causing my f*cks to be depleted
To the point you couldn't
Receive them

Your love
You could not see him

I regret
That I ever opened my mouth
To try to inspire
And take you higher
Towards the goals that you desired
Gaining the accomplishments you acquired
While my wants never conspired
And my body grew tired
While your mistakes
Put out my fire

Excuse me
For ever wanting to be loved
And thinking it only fair
To receive kisses and hugs
Instead of attitude and shoulder shrugs
Punches and two handed shoves
Fist fights and cursing
Instead of affection
Your behavior was aversive

My bad
That I was a great dad
And a man that 98% of women in your position
Wish they had
And for being glad
To receive your half-a** effort
And for being your umbrella
In rainy weather
And never thinking that I could do better

Yes, it's my fault
That I was so d*mn dedicated
And every pain you had
I tried my best to medicate it
Always worked a full time job
While also working to be highly educated
Moved mountains
To try to make sure everything you did for me
Never went uncompensated

Forgive me please
Because I wanted someone
That would make my life worth living
And wanted to take from a relationship
The same things I was giving in
I thought it was a given
But maybe it's just a fairy tale
I wanted to live in

I guess I should be ashamed of me
For wanting to be viewed as a king
In the eyes of a woman
I viewed as my queen
Actually, was it too much to be treated merely
Like a human being

I guess I should not have believed in dreams

Maybe I'm a little too arty
For believing in love that can be hearty
So, for my figmented expectation
Of our relationship
What I am trying to say
If I have been saying anything at all
Is this

...

"I'm sorry."

Revelation

The voyage from the valley to the peak
From seed to the tree
From earth to the sky
Bottom to the top
Cold to the hot
1 to 100%
Nothing to something
Poor to rich
Child to adult
Juvenile to mature
Failure to success
Dehydrated to quenched
Basic to advanced
Hungry to filled
Walking to running
Slow to fast
None to all
Future from past
From limits to infinite
Birth to death
Then, death to eternal life
...
Is never a straight line.

After waking up
And seeing that the sun still shines
I learned that the world keeps going
No matter what problems arise
Even mine

And now my mind
Releases the thoughts of the previous crime
That occurred inside of yesterday's time

Moving on to the next page of my life
I feel crucified like I was jesus christ
Because I feel more like him
After being sacrificed
By a person I love
Who thought so selfishly
But as I hung I wondered
"Why has she forsaken me?"

And at this moment I have died
And now god has taken me

My soul was Hers and she did not care
She had eyes but could not see
And ears that could not hear

I looked in the mirror today
And the cracks had vanished
The image was clear
I saw that I was still here
I was still breathing
Even though she was not near

Then I made the decision
That I would no longer care
I was no longer there

Inside a place of dissolution
I have now found my solution
Raised an internal revolution

I am the sun dawning on a new experience
I have been behind clouds
And they have caused a large interference

But I now have clearance to shine
With the appearance of a divine
One of a kind
Mind
Trying to find
What lies within the lines of my rhymes

I now sit on solid ground
For I was blind but now I see
And I was lost,
But now I am found

Ashe.

Squeeze Her tightly
But allow Her to go
If she returns to you nighlty
Then, that's how you will know.

Looking out my window
I have amazing views
I use my past
To realize the last
Struggle deployed
Grew me
After I destroyed it
Instead of it destroying me.

Within the dot
There is a line
The line is this life of mine
It extends its length in search to find
Its end is somewhere within my timeline
It grows longer from the lessons learned behind
Its growth is never straight
More like wild vines.

It only took 13 years to reach enough
13 days to realize we had depleted love
In 13 hours, I moved all of my stuff
Then, 13 minutes after
I realized you will make this tough

13 weeks went by, since the day I left
You began harassing me
I took 13 breathes
In 13 hours cops came to your doorstep
13 minutes later they made the arrest

13 days later, 13 calls came back to back
All 13 calls ignored, I did not react
After 13 calls on top of that
I picked up and heard, "I want you back."

I replied, "In 13 years, I figured it out
The last 13 months taught me what love is about
If she is not within, you can't give Her out
So I looked in 13 mirrors and I see Her now…"

…

"…And none of the 13 reflections were you."

You are my ex
An X over every memory we shared
Every picture you were in
Every smile and grin

You are my ex
The X that was over my happiness
Over my joy
Covered my peace
And through my life

You are my ex
The two X's I had for eyes
Because I was dead with you
The ex in extinct
As in the love we shared

You are my ex
The X that marks the time in my life
I do not want to remember
And the X that reminds me of what to forget

You are my ex
The X next to my signature
On the divorce papers
And the X I used to revise this poem

You are my ex
The X tattooed over my heart
So another woman can find the treasure you lost
And your X will mark the spot.

They described Her
In the bible
Her value worth more than gold

Her voice was soft
As baby birds' chirps
Her fragrance sweet and bold

Her feeling was silk
Woven by larva
Her body molded by god

Her breast were full
Nourished the earth
Her arms stretched abroad

Her core was wisdom,
Knowledge and power
Her acquisition was life's end

Her beauty was blinding
Her smile fulfilled
All that I desire
She transcends

I thought she was you
And you were Her
But found your reflection to be blurred

Because whatever we shared
My vision was impaired
I now see that it is not you
And this is not Her.

It's all your fault
Blame is yours by default
Locked in a vault
Is the truth behind the assault
But halt
...
Even if you were to exalt
Above the asphalt
It would still be
All your fault.

- from Her POV

The colors have faded away
It's now time to return to a gray.

I
See
Your
True
Colors
Through
You.

The sea gives itself to me
In the broken seashells along the shore
In the pelican's glide above
And among the seagulls hovering around kids
with bread below

The beach kisses me on my skin
As the sun's rays massage their way
Into my melanin
And entices me visually
Within the palm tree leaves
Dancing in the constant cool breeze

A flock of Crows echo in my ear drum
As they move from branch to light pole
The tide pulls and pushes me
As it cycles from high to low

The white crushed shells within the sand
Finds there way in between everything
As I rummage for treasures of the sea

I look down into the water and spot
Horseshoe crabs cautiously crawling
Within the seaweed

The shallows fulfills my curiosity
To see what lies beneath

Sand prints from many birds
Still imprinted into the moist clay
At the water's edge

The waves repeatedly taps at its limits
Like the soft tap on an African drum

The rhythm it creates seems to to be
The baseline for all of the other sounds
I hear

I find a palm size fragment of a shell
That was called home to some creature
In the past

And I reposition it in my hand
As I then toss it where the water
Is calm

Six skips upon the ocean's surface
Then it plunges into the ocean's deep

Now living with the only purpose of
Making it back to the ocean's shore
Once more.

Look Up
When they pull you down
Stay focus
On where you are headed now
Not turned around
Staring at the footprints in the ground.

It is real
Embrace it
Understand it
Learn it

Don't react to it
And don't run from it.

I am me
I am not you
I am not them
I am not him
I am not Her
I am me.

No one eye
Can see
What your two eyes
Can't.

After grey clouds recede
Blue skies appear

After lightning strikes
It is thunder you hear

Where birth exist
Death follows after

The cage is made
To hold something captured

Lions will be lions
And tigers will be tigers

If a lie is not aborted
You will conceive a liar

Where there is an in
There is also an out

To get from A to B
There are many routes

While young
Embrace mistakes, heartbreaks, and earthquakes

When old
Use your bruises and scars to create

Nothing in life is guaranteed

But there are some things
That we can call certainties.

To all negative and bad vibes
Here is a kiss (muah)

Goodbye.

Love
is
a
~~Word~~
**Her.**

# Resurrection

I dip Her underneath
The surface of a sacred pool
Symbolizing me relinquishing Her
Into the hands of gods
To be cleansed
To be sanctified
To be healed
Lifting Her from the water's depths
I retrieve Her from the universe
As we reunite anew.

I have guarded
My half-a-heart
So that it will not be
Torn


Apart


Again.

I was married my entire adult life
All I know is how to give love
To a wife

...

Are you that somebody?

Moments when you want sex
And the only one that returns your text
Is your ex

...

No other prospects.
(The single life is so complex)

I like Her
But I love Her
I talk to Her
But I f*ck Her
I chill with Her
And I go out with Her
I make love to Her
But I only tease Her
I call Her
But I text Her
I work with Her
I only had one night with Her
I flirt with Her
I fight with Her
She likes it when I cuddle Her
I kiss Her
I'm sick of Her
I live with Her
But I visit Her
...
Why am I searching for Her
In the midst of blurs?

While you are here
Go
Downtown
Uptown
East side
West side

Spend time in
Queens
Bronx
LIC
Brooklyn

Explore
Inwood
Midtown
Chelsea
Harlem

Then enjoy
The village
The heights
The bridges
And parks

But also save time
To visit
My heart.

Candles lit
Romantic sh*t
Passionate
Licks on clit
Tongue flicks
Taste so rich
Body clinch
Inhibit movement
P*ssy wet
Leaking faucet
Perfect fit
Intimate
Deposit d*ck
Into it
Intricate
Stimulant
Fleshly composite
Soft Plump lips
So delicate
Pink exquisite
Pleasure implicit
Adequate d*ck
Causing you to be inarticulate
Sexually literate
Physically magnet
Spiritually orbit
Mouth filled with (shhhhhh)....Quiet
Suckage on it
Downtown trip
Salivating moist drip
Stroke, suck, lick, then spit
Glistening shaft and tip
White ejaculate
Swallowed all of it

We exhibit
The subtle art of being
Anti-celibate.

You turn me on
And I turn you on too
So let's do
What the f*ck we want to
You are questioning if it's too soon
At the most inopportune time
...
Naked on the bed
In this hotel room.

I don't give a damn what you may think
I'm not buying another
Motherf*cking drink
For a girl with a cute smile
And bright eyes
That looks my way and winks
If she has closed thighs
She is going to be dry f*cking with me

I don't give a damn how much she blinks
I'm not buying another
Motherf*cking drink
Because these drinks are expensive as sh*t
And these nights are as lonely as it gets
I will not be hoodwinked a bit
Flushing my hard earned money down the sink

I'm not buying another motherf*cking drink
So if you want a drink out of me
You must be willing to f*ck
Because that's the only way
My wallet is giving this money up
I don't give a damn what you may think
I'm not buying another
Motherf*cking drink.


...


- written while alone, drunk, and lost

It doesn't make sense how I feel
But the pain is real
Maybe the contents of this glass
Can fill this everlasting void
Or maybe these pills will.

(Searching for my antidote)

Where am I?
The rustling in the trees
Who's there?
The loud cries of an unrecognized creature
What is that?
In the river it appears
In my reflection.

Is this Her?
Or is she just another
Imitated lover
For me to be Her lover
To then discover
While under my covers
She was undercover
And not Her.

Remind me
Convince me
Advise me
Help me
I'm currently
Forgetting the point of Her.

"I don't want you
To give your all

I want everything else
After you have given to yourself."

Growth out of my consciousness
Thoughts grown from cognizance
Bath in the universe
Immersed inside of my providence

Healing hurts as a consequence
Submerge inside of confidence
Meditate in the galaxy
Be free with all cautiousness

Exercise my dominance
Never walk away profit less
Mind empty but still present
Don't lessen it as thoughtlessness

Transform into anonymous
Worry becomes obsolesce
Escape from your reality
Finally, I'm autonomous.

I met Her in the Summer
When my heart was in Winter
I am sprung by the Spring
When I Autumn in Her with you.

The sunsets
But then rises
So it's no surprise when
You say you are doing better now

I knew where we were headed
Was only producing an outcome
We would have dreaded
And we would have regretted
The decision to not turn back around

I know your preference
Would have been for us to stay together
But my conscious did not want this
To relinquish a better life for the future
By allowing actions to continue
That could have changed our lives forever
Instead it decided to forecast
Our future like the weather
And saw that leaving
Would give an outcome better
Than the path that we were headed down

So I hope we can retain remnants
Of our love through a friendship
And be happy for each other's happiness
Overlooking our past hardship

And relationship

We know it was a necessity
A needed ingredient inside of a recipe
For you and me
To be
Better now.

I was contaminated
From being given poison
And having it shoved down my throat
It slowly ate away
At my insides
But then Her lips were my antidote

I had an infection
In my love
I didn't know how I got it
But the first time
Her eyes stared at me
I received antibiotics

I suffered with
Intense migraines back then
Now I have no pain at all
It seems the more
I tapped into Her mind
The more Her thoughts became my Tylenol

I had contracted a broken heart
Physicians said
It was something they had never seen
No one had any answers
Until i was given
Her body as a vaccine

There was an ulcer in my soul
Internal bleeding
Related to alcohol
But all symptoms
Have subsided
Her skin was pepto-bismol

I had burns, cuts,
And puncture wounds
Scabs all over my precious organs
But then Her touch
Was applied on me
Her hands were neosporin

My pain is cured
My sickness relieved
Remedies from our conversations
Now that I have Her in my life
I am forever healed
Because she is my medication.

Her eyes were on me constantly

Her lips were on me tenderly

Her hands caressed me softly

Her body pressed against me roughly

Her thoughts were on me deeply

Her skin was on me smoothly

Her hair touched me gently

Her fingers gripped me tightly

Her voice called me loudly

Her legs wrapped around me firmly

Her heart beat for me quickly

Her cum came for me intensely

Her existence is in me, completely.

"I don't want all of you
For myself

I want everything left
After you have first
Given to yourself."

Her mind
Her body
Her soul
Is mine.

Anew

My sun is on an infinite rise
Rising but never setting in the skies
She rises, dark dies
Night never comes
And my cloud
No longer cries.

I can't wait to take off my shirt
Showing the scars from my hurt
But Letting the vitamin D filled radiation
Penetrate my melaninated hue
Causing an excavation of my dirt
While tanning this crimson-filled
Brown covered anatomy
Metaphorically
She is a cardiovascular remedy
To my heart's complications
I'm remembering
Every word when Me and my sun
Established solar conversation
As my view of Her and Her sight of me
Builds a relationship
That is demanded by me the planet
And she the center of my universe
As I orbit around it
While Her gravity pulls me
And moves me with Her revolving domination
I am stranded in this spatial contemplation of it
I am handed the stars within my optics
To manage my own galactic revelation
I have access to Her worth
While standing on earth feeling new
Skies are blue
My rebirth occurs
And the past pain is burnt in the heat of my sun
From the very first sight of it over our horizon
My eyes are drawn to Her grin
My worries are gone because I then
Get to see Her once again
...
At Dawn.

I am the Dawn
And she is me
My hair reaches out like Her rays
As she shines upon me

I rise as she rises
The morning exist because of us
Our interaction is an erection
This resurrection is amorous

She is my Dawn
And I am Her day
We meet in the sky
Our existence together is interplay.

She was not Her
And being nothing like she,
You are now Her.

The sun came across the horizon
Kissed my skin and left it's lipstick there
The black darkness that overshadowed me
Has vanished because she entered where
The stars lit my life at night
But now I know the love they share
With me was only because of she
The one that's sitting next to me in Her chair.

If she is my sun
Then my sun is Her.

The crackling of the wood
Nothing can duplicate
The blaze dancing on old trees

The smell emitted from the embers
Warmth produced by flames
The orange glow casted on brown skin

The ambience it creates for lovers
Cuddles in the winter cold
We admire
The performance of a simple fire in place.

My foundation holds a story
Giving my past the glory
Growth and Knowledge
Is my future
And my future is my past
As well as
My task to make
Using my past to create my future
By omitting my past mistakes
I build my fate on Her
The one that lives in me
And on Her I stand
Knowing my future exist presently.

My words
Glorify your mind
My thoughts
Honor your soul
My hands
Praise your skin.

She was Her eyes
Glistening in the dim light of this lounge
She was Her hands
Insulated by my palms
As I wrapped them around Hers
She was Her shoulders
That were cocoa buttery glowing
Beyond Her shirt
She was Her thighs
That were overlapping
With Her almond complexion
Seeping out of Her skirt
She was the large hoop earrings
That rested on Her shoulders and cheeks
She was Her thoughts
As she stared at me, while thinking so deep
She was Her voice
As it released Her ideas into my soul
She was the candle flame
Dancing on the table
Dressed in orange and gold
She was Her lips
As she applied balm evenly
And pressed them together
She was Her smile
Bright and luminescent in this dark room
She was Her food
As she properly cut and consumed
She was beautiful
As she sat across from me in Her chair
She was everything to me
Without Her ever being there.

Absent is the sound from my mouth
Mute as the beat of my heart
Underneath my flesh
My obsession for this silence
Reveals the underlying passion
The hidden essence of love

Quiet is my motions
Secretly approaching the Mystery
Of being devoured by the blanket
Cast from beneath your outer layer

The flavor of silk
Milked from the pores of my fascination
Patience for the period that has past
Wasting time obsessed
By your blessed presence
Without words being spoken

I am Speechless.

I have followed a path into to a foreign land
As I stand on a ground made of sand
To be fed by the works of my hand
My plan is one of grand scale
One similar to old fairy tales
Where a protagonist rises and does not fail
And lives happily ever after
After he prevails.

Real eyes
Realize
Real lies
Bona fide
Authentic
Raw
Unsynthesized
Love in the pure
Growth supersized
Chasing you far
I seek and you hide
In me you confide
In you I reside
Grass is always greener
When it's grown the inside
Abide with the tide
The tide falls and rise
Triumphant we are
But it starts with a try
The tears that you cry
Are not from your eye
It comes from the past
Full of pain and deprive
But now you know me
Now you're alive
Who would've thought
That you were already by my side
We will die as we ride
We will fly as we're high
Say hi to your love
And tell the pain "bye"
Because she is here now
She is genuine.

Redefine

Authentic words communicating out of me
To introduce you to my reality
So that my views may be used
To develop and create
A multitude of other galaxies.

"No more
Do I fit into your boxes or labels
Your heart, devices
Or your cables

I am free."

In the eyes of love
Is both dusk and Dawn
Both happiness and pain
Both growth and death

In the eyes of love
Is both the moon and the sun
Both blue skies and the rain
Both more and less

In the eyes of love
Is both the knight and the pawn
Both the guilt and the shame
Both your worst and your best

In the eyes of love
Is both boredom and fun
Both wild and tame
Both calm and stress

In the eyes of love
Is Me.

There is no bending spoon
You bend
There is no air in exhaustion
You are a program
You function on 0s and 1s
Putting out what you put in
The rabbit hole goes as deep
As you are willing to deepen
Is life real or just a dream
That you live in?
Red or Green
She has chosen.

My eyes have closed
But
Eyes
Still see
You.

I detached from the wing of a bird in flight
Then I was carried by the wind to new heights
Drifting
Floating
Soaring
Across the sea and land
With nothing guiding my destiny
Except the wind
I experienced the life of the weightless
Attached to nothing but myself
I was faithless
And I was fate-less
While also trace-less
Unidentified
The extinction of time
I was ageless
Headed in every direction
I was aimless
Nothing held me down
Nor up
Except
Myself.

In and out of my life
Some things have went
But the most important
Has remained.

One of them
Is Her.

Remember,
You are a we
Not an I.

- note to self

With a mirror between us two
I tell you everything
You already knew
I am grateful
For the things that we do
There is only one us
There is only one you
I never knew
Your true value
Until all I had left was you
You are the residue
Left behind for my rescue
The discovery of who I am
You are my breakthrough
You kept me together
Cemented my essence
You are my glue
I now know love
Something I thought I already knew
But you never do
Until she
Is in the mirror
Staring back at you.

*From birth*
*To disasters*
*To happily ever afters,*
*With* Her.

# Birth

*Lover, 1*
*Herman, 3*
*A Book By its Cover, 5*
*Ovulation, 7*
*Dot, 9*
*Mother Love, 11*
*Beautiful I, 13*
*Wave, 15*
*My Dawn, 17*
*Hero, 19*
*>Friend, 21*
*Impatience, 23*

# Adolescence

*Butterflies, 27*
*Mondrian, 29*
*3am, 31*
*A Kiss of Red, 33*
*Please Wait, 35*
*High, 37*
*Divine Rewind, 39*
*Sunset, 41*
*A Fish in the Sea, 43*
*Beautiful II, 45*
*Need Her, 47*
*Heat, 49*
*Seasoned, 51*
*Sand, 53*
*Sharing Water, 55*
*All, 57*

# Growth

*Empty Promise, 59*
*Forecast, 61*
*Reverse, 63*
*That Those, 65*
*The Audacity to Love, 67*
*Beautiful III, 71*
*3love, 73*
*Black Hole, 75*
*Half, 77*
*You Two, 79*
*Braid, 81*
*Cumxwithxme, 83*
*Blue, 85*
*I Can't Keep, 87*
*Keel, 89*
*Wait for it, 91*
*The Bliss of An Obsession, 93*

# Death

*Gradient, 99*
*Sunset at Dawn, 101*
*Black Horizon, 103*
*Once Upon A Time, 105*
*Empty Bottle, 109*
*Drinker, 111*
*Crimson Tide, 113*
*5050, 115*
*Pyre, 117*
*I am Evil, 119*
*Oxymoron, 121*
*Gold Plated, 123*
*Meant for Me, 125*
*Reflectionless, 127*
*No More, 129*
*Evil, 131*
*Right and Wrong, 133*
*Where It Hurts, 135*
*Let Go, 137*
*Have You Ever?, 139*
*Destroyed, 145*
*F\*cker, 147*
*Perf Ex, 149*
*Dungeon, 151*
*To Her, 153*
*Forgive & Forget?, 157*
*Sorry, 159*

# Revelation

*A to B, 165*
*Revelation 23, Verse 1, 167*
*Holder, 171*
*Views, 173*
*Timeline, 175*
*13, 177*
*X, 179*
*This Ain't Her, 181*
*Fault, 183*
*Grayscale, 185*
*Transparent, 187*
*The Ocean's Shore, 189*
*Forward, 193*
*Pain, 195*
*Me, 197*
*MJ, 199*
*Certainties, 201*
*Good Vibes Only, 203*
*Love, 205*

# Resurrection

*Ablution, 207*
*Guardian, 209*
*Are You That Somebody?, 211*
*Cuffing Season, 213*
*In the Midst of Blurs, 215*
*Just Another NY Attraction, 217*
*Anti-Celibate, 219*
*Hotel room, 223*
*Not Another, 225*
*Antidote, 227*
*Unrecognized, 229*
*Is This Her?, 231*
*The Point, 233*
*You First, 235*
*Green Meditation, 237*
*Four Seasons, 239*
*Better Now, 241*
*Doctor, 243*
*Lee, 247*
*First, You, 249*
*Her is Mine, 251*

# Anew

*Forever Dawn, 253*
*A New Day, 255*
*Dawn and Eye, 257*
*You are Her, 259*
*Sunnier, 261*
*Sun, 263*
*Fireplace, 265*
*Wiser, 267*
*Extol, 269*
*She Was Nothing, 271*
*Speechless, 273*
*Conqueror, 275*
*Real, 277*

# Redefine

*Purpose, 279*
*Transcendence, 281*
*The Eyes of Love, 283*
*Mr. Anderson, 285*
*Still See, 287*
*Weightless, 289*
*Remainder, 291*
*We, 293*
*I Love Her, 295*
*Her, 297*

# From the Author

(HER) is a love story that poetically narrates my personal pursuit of love. Within these pages, I have placed the feelings, emotions, thoughts, pain, hate, forgiveness, regret, and conclusions that I acquired over my lifetime. My hope is that my experiences and the way I expressed them will help others find, feel, and understand self love as the origin of all other love in life.

(HER) is also a poetic thesis. Using the pronoun "Her" in reference to many different entities, my intent is to pose the idea of love being a diety with the same ambiguity of gods in major religions. In fact, I believe love is the catalyst concept that creates religions and their gods. So through poetry, I want people to see love as an idea, not an action or a tangible object that we give to people, but rather an omnipresent entity that is found inside of everything existing.

Furthermore, our pursuit of this love should not be external, but rather a journey of the spirit, taking place within. And only there is where you will find Her.

Thank you to all of my relationships and the people I've built them with.

And thank you for reading this.

- tonii

*E: tonii@toniiinc.com*
*IG: @tonii2eyes*

Made in the USA
Middletown, DE
19 November 2021